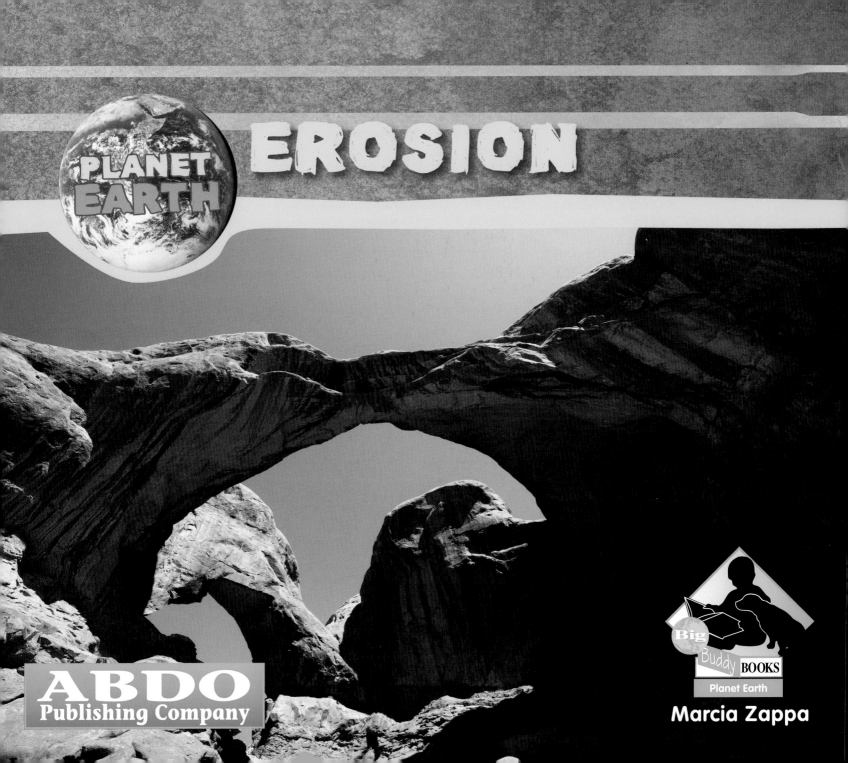

EROSION

PLANET EARTH

ABDO
Publishing Company

Big Buddy BOOKS
Planet Earth

Marcia Zappa

VISIT US AT
www.abdopublishing.com

Published by ABDO Publishing Company, 8000 West 78th Street, Edina, Minnesota 55439.

Copyright © 2011 by Abdo Consulting Group, Inc. International copyrights reserved in all countries. No part of this book may be reproduced in any form without written permission from the publisher. Big Buddy Books™ is a trademark and logo of ABDO Publishing Company.

Printed in the United States of America, North Mankato, Minnesota.
032010
092010
♻ PRINTED ON RECYCLED PAPER

Coordinating Series Editor: Rochelle Baltzer
Contributing Editors: Heidi M.D. Elston, Megan M. Gunderson, BreAnn Rumsch, Sarah Tieck
Graphic Design: Adam Craven
Cover Photograph: *Shutterstock*: Galyna Andrushko.
Interior Photographs/Illustrations: *iStockphoto*: ©iStockphoto.com/dgrilla (p. 5), ©iStockphoto.com/gcosoveanu (p. 29); NASA (p. 5); *Peter Arnold, Inc.*: Patrick Neri/Digital Light Source (p. 17), *Photo Researchers, Inc.*: Tom Burnside (p. 25), Fletcher & Baylis (p. 21), Tom Myers (p. 21), Susan Rayfield (p. 11), Leonard Lee Rue III (p. 19), James Steinberg (p. 9), Michael Szoenyi (p. 5), Terry Whittaker (p. 5); *Shutterstock*: Ramunas Bruzas (p. 15), Dainis Deries (p. 23), Anton Foltin (p. 7), Markus Gann (p. 23), Jorg Hackermann (p. 30), Christopher Jones (p. 21), kohy (p. 19), Phillip Lange (p. 13), Ales Liska (p. 27), Dr. Morley Read (p. 19), TTphoto (p. 27).

Library of Congress Cataloging-in-Publication Data

Zappa, Marcia, 1985-
  Erosion / Marcia Zappa.
    p. cm. -- (Planet Earth)
  ISBN 978-1-61613-491-4
  1. Erosion--Juvenile literature. I. Title.
QE571.Z37 2011
551.3'02--dc22
                    2009053194

TABLE OF CONTENTS

EARTH-SHAPING POWER

Planet Earth is an amazing place. From towering mountains to deep oceans, natural wonders are all around. Many forces and **processes** shape Earth. One important process is erosion.

During erosion, small pieces of rock and soil break away from Earth. Then, natural forces such as wind, water, and **gravity** step in. They move the pieces to new locations.

Erosion creates many of Earth's interesting landforms.

Erosion changes Earth's land. It wears down mountain peaks and carves out valleys. It builds up lowlands and fills in riverbeds. Generally, erosion is a slow process. Thousands of years may pass before its powerful effects can be seen. But sometimes, erosion can have immediate effects.

BREAKING UP

Erosion begins when pieces of rock and soil break away from Earth. This **process** is called weathering. The two main types of weathering are mechanical and chemical.

Rock may seem hard and strong. But, weathering can break it apart.

POUNDING AWAY

Mechanical weathering changes a rock's size. It breaks rock into pieces. But it does not change the inner makeup of a rock.

Freezing water is one common cause of mechanical weathering. When water turns to ice, it swells. Sometimes, water flows into tiny cracks in rock. If it freezes, it can swell so much that the rock breaks apart!

Weathering caused by freezing water is called frost wedging.

Water in ice form is about 10 percent larger than water in liquid form.

11

Wind, water, and **glaciers** are moving forces that cause mechanical weathering. Wind breaks off pieces of **landforms** as it blows by. Rivers and glaciers wear down land as they move over it.

Sometimes, wind, water, and glaciers carry pieces of rock and soil with them. These moving pieces hit against Earth's surface, weathering it even more.

Ocean waves weather coastlines.

13

CHANGING FORM

Chemical weathering changes the inner makeup of rocks. Sometimes, it changes a rock into a different type of rock. Chemical reactions cause this type of weathering. These reactions often break apart or **dissolve** rocks.

Many caves are formed by chemical weathering. Water and other liquids dissolve rock, leaving behind a cave.

SCIENCE SPOT

Acid rain forms when water in the air mixes with gases. These gases are often from air pollution.

Chemical weathering can happen in several ways. Some rocks, such as salt, **dissolve** in water. Many rocks can be dissolved by acid rain. Other rocks mix with air to form something new. This **process** is called oxidation.

16

Oxidation creates red stripes in the hills of South Dakota's Badlands National Park.

MOVING PIECES

After pieces of rock and soil break apart, they often move to new locations. Flowing rivers carry the pieces toward the ocean. **Glaciers** pick them up and slowly move them downhill. Wind also carries them to new areas.

Glaciers move very slowly. Erosion caused by glaciers usually takes thousands of years.

The pieces of rock and soil carried by a river are called its load. A river's load can make it look different colors, such as green, yellow, or brown.

SCIENCE SPOT

Glaciers can carry large pieces of rock. Sometimes, these rocks scratch Earth's surface as they drag slowly along. The lines they leave behind are called striations.

MASS WASTING

The effects of erosion are usually gradual. Yet sometimes they are **extreme**. This is often true of mass wasting, such as landslides. Mass wasting can harm people, animals, plants, and land.

Mass wasting happens when **gravity** moves soil and rock downhill. This can happen quickly after events that loosen the ground. For example, earthquakes, heavy rain, and poorly planned building can cause landslides.

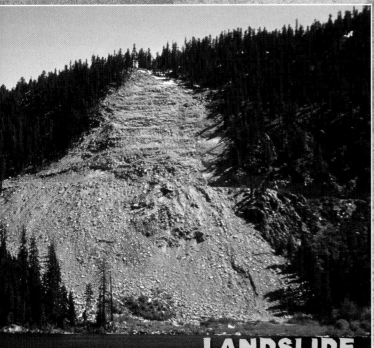

LANDSLIDE

Rockfalls are a common type of mass wasting. Sometimes, weathering breaks rock away from a hill or a mountainside. Then, it falls to the ground.

ROCKFALL

FLOW

Flows are similar to landslides, but they move slower. And, flows usually occur when heavy rains weather a hillside.

CHANGING THE WORLD

Erosion is constantly changing Earth's surface. Over time, erosion creates **landforms**. It carves out valleys and canyons. It also wears down mountains and builds up lowlands.

Erosion's effects can be good. By breaking up rock, erosion helps create soil. People need soil to grow crops and plants. This supports life on Earth.

From sea cliffs (*above*) to sand dunes (*left*), the effects of erosion can look very different.

Erosion can also be harmful. A landslide can destroy homes and bury roads. And, erosion washes away farming soil. It can also create deep ditches called gullies. Gullies ruin fields by making them too small to farm.

Gullies form when too much water flows through soil.

25

CAREFUL LAND USE

Erosion is a natural process. But, activities such as farming and logging can speed it up unnaturally. Plants and trees shield rock and soil from erosion. When farmers and loggers clear land, erosion is more likely to occur.

Farmers clear land to grow crops.

Loggers cut down trees to make lumber.

People work to control unnatural erosion. Farmers **shield** soil by keeping fields covered with plants. And, loggers obey laws about where they can cut down trees.

You can help too! Recycle paper to reduce the number of trees cut down. And, use hiking trails and sidewalks to avoid disturbing natural areas. These actions help keep Earth a beautiful place!

Erosion plays an important part in creating Earth's natural wonders!

29

DOWN TO EARTH:
A FEW MORE FACTS ABOUT EROSION

- Weathering caused by living things is called biotic weathering. This name comes from the word *bio*, which means "life."
- Temperature changes can cause mechanical weathering. Rock swells when warmed and contracts when cooled. This can weaken rock and cause it to fall apart. In the desert (*right*), hot days and cold nights turn rock into sand.
- Weathering affects different types of rock in different ways. How a rock is affected depends on its inner makeup.

IMPORTANT WORDS

dissolve (dih-ZAHLV) to become part of a liquid.

extreme (ihk-STREEM) far beyond the usual.

glacier (GLAY-shuhr) a huge chunk of ice and snow on land.

gravity a natural force that pulls objects to the ground.

landform a natural feature of a land surface. Hills and mountains are types of landforms.

process a natural order of actions.

shield (SHEELD) to provide a cover that guards against harm or danger.

WEB SITES

To learn more about erosion, visit ABDO Publishing Company online. Web sites about erosion are featured on our Book Links page. These links are routinely monitored and updated to provide the most current information available.

www.abdopublishing.com

INDEX